HOW TO START A PROFITABLE FOOD TRUCK BUSINESS FOR BEGINNERS

The Essentials Of Food Truck Management

Sophia Williams

Copyright Page

Author: Sophia Williams

Copyright © [2024] by [Sophia Williams]

All rights reserved.

No part of this book may be reproduced, stored in a retrieval system, or transmitted in any form or by any means, electronic, mechanical, photocopying, recording, or otherwise, without the prior written permission of the publisher, except in the case of brief quotations embodied in critical articles or reviews and certain other noncommercial uses permitted by copyright law.

This book is a work of nonfiction. Names, characters, places, and incidents either are products of the author's imagination or are used fictitiously. Any resemblance to actual events, locales, or persons, living or dead, is entirely coincidental.

Disclaimer:

The advice and strategies contained herein may not be suitable for every situation. This work is sold with the understanding that neither the author nor the publisher is engaged in rendering legal, accounting, or other professional services. If professional assistance is required, the services of a competent professional person should be sought. The author and publisher specifically disclaim any liability that is incurred from the use or application of the contents of this book.

Table of Contents

HOW TO START A PROFITABLE FOOD TRUCK BUSINESS FOR BEGINNERS 1
    Credits: 8
INTRODUCTION 9
    Embarking on Your Food Truck Journey 9
    The Evolution of Food Trucks 10
    Why Choose a Food Truck? 11
    What This Book Covers 12
Chapter 1 14
    Laying the Foundation 14
Chapter 2 25
    Legalities and Logistics 25
    Legal Requirements 26
    Logistical Considerations 29
Chapter 3 33
    Designing and Outfitting your Food Truck 33
    Choosing and Customizing Your Truck 34
    Branding Your Food Truck 36
Chapter 4 39
    Menu Development and Operations 39
    Crafting Your Menu 40
        Balancing Creativity and Cost 41
        Sourcing Quality Ingredients 41

Pricing Your Menu Items 42
Day-to-Day Operations 43
    Inventory Management................................44
    Scheduling and Staffing 44
    Efficient Service Practices 45
Chapter 5 47
    Marketing and customer engagement 47
    Your Truck Branding 48
- Name 48
- Logo 48
- Tagline 48
- Colors and Fonts 49
    Consistent Brand Messaging 49
    Truck Design and Presentation 49
    Social Media Marketing................................50
    Choosing the Right Platforms........................50
- Instagram 51
- Facebook 51
- Twitter 51
- TikTok 51
- Pinterest 51
    Creating Engaging Content 51
    High-Quality Photos 52
    Behind-the-Scenes 52

Customer Spotlights 52
Promotions and Specials 52
Events and Locations 52
Leveraging User-Generated Content 53
Engaging with Your Audience 53
Social Media Advertising 53
Promotions and Events 54
Limited-Time Offers and Specials 54
Loyalty Programs 55
Event Participation 55
Hosting Your Own Events 56
- Launch Parties 56
- Themed Nights 56
- Cooking Demonstrations 56

Collaborations and Partnerships 57
Customer Loyalty Programs 57
Types of Loyalty Programs 57
1. Points-Based Programs 58
2. Punch Cards 58
3. Tiered Programs 58
4. Referral Programs 58

Implementing a Digital Loyalty Program 58
Personalizing Customer Interactions 59
Customer Feedback and Reviews 59

- Encouraging Customer Feedback 60
- Responding to Reviews 60
- Using Feedback for Improvement 61
- Showcasing Positive Reviews 61

Community Involvement 62
- Supporting Local Causes 62
- Participating in Community Events 62

Marketing Analytics and Measurement 64
- Setting Marketing Goals 64
- Tracking Key Metrics 65
  - Sales Revenue 65
  - Customer Acquisition 65
  - Customer Retention 65
  - Social Media Engagement 66
  - Website Traffic 66
  - Email Marketing Performance 66
- Analyzing Data and Making Adjustments 66
- A/B Testing 67
- Search Engine Optimization (SEO) 67
- Keyword Research 68
- On-Page Optimization 68
- Local SEO 68
- Content Marketing 68
- Email Marketing 69

- Online Advertising 69
- Offline Marketing Strategies 70
  - Flyers and Posters 70
  - Business Cards 70
  - Local Media 71
  - Networking 71
- Customer Engagement Techniques 72
  - Personalization 72
  - Customer Surveys 73
  - Interactive Experiences 73
    - Cooking Demonstrations 74
    - Photo Opportunities 74
    - Games and Contests 74
  - Exceptional Customer Service 74
- Chapter 6 75
- Growth Strategies and Financial Management of a Food Truck Business 75
  - Growth Strategies 76
    - Market Research and Niche Identification 76
    - Strategic Location Planning 77
    - Branding and Marketing 77
    - Menu Innovation 78
    - Expansion and Diversification 79
  - Financial Management 79
    - Budgeting and Forecasting 79

Cost Control 80
Pricing Strategy 81
Cash Flow Management 81
Financial Reporting and Analysis 82
Tax Compliance and Planning 83
CONCLUSION 86
The Road Ahead 86
Sample Food Truck Business Plan 92
Glossary of Terms 100

Credits:

Special thanks to You! (The Buyer). Your Purchase is highly Appreciated.

INTRODUCTION
Embarking on Your Food Truck Journey

In recent years, food trucks have evolved from a niche trend into a culinary revolution. These mobile kitchens have become a staple in urban landscapes and rural festivals alike, offering gourmet meals, fusion cuisine, and traditional comfort food to a diverse and ever-growing clientele. The allure of the food truck business lies in its combination of culinary creativity and entrepreneurial spirit, providing a unique platform for aspiring chefs and business owners to showcase their talent without the substantial overheads of a traditional restaurant.

This book, " How to start a successful food truck business," is designed to be your comprehensive companion on the exciting journey of launching and running a successful food truck. Whether you're a seasoned chef looking to break free from the confines of a brick-and-mortar establishment or a passionate foodie with dreams of sharing your culinary creations with the world, this guide will equip you with the knowledge and tools necessary to turn your vision into a thriving reality.

The Evolution of Food Trucks

To understand the food truck phenomenon, it's essential to appreciate its history and evolution. The concept of mobile food vending dates back centuries, but the modern food truck movement began in the early 2000s in cities like Los Angeles and New York. These early pioneers capitalized on social media to attract followers and create buzz, transforming food trucks into a viable business model and cultural icon. Today, food trucks are a billion-dollar industry, contributing to the vibrant tapestry of local economies and food cultures around the world.

Why Choose a Food Truck?

There are numerous reasons why starting a food truck can be an appealing business venture:

1. **Lower Startup Costs**: Compared to opening a restaurant, the initial investment for a food truck is significantly lower. This makes it an accessible option for many aspiring entrepreneurs.
2. **Flexibility and Mobility**: A food truck allows you to bring your cuisine directly to your customers, whether at festivals, farmers' markets, or city streets. This mobility can lead to greater market exposure and diverse revenue streams.
3. **Creative Freedom**: Running a food truck provides a platform to experiment with menu items and culinary concepts, allowing for a dynamic and responsive approach to customer preferences.
4. **Community Engagement**: Food trucks often become integral parts of the communities they serve, fostering connections and loyal customer bases through regular interactions and participation in local events.

What This Book Covers

" How to start a successful food truck business " is structured to guide you through every stage of the food truck business journey, from conceptualization to operational success. Here's a brief overview of what you can expect to learn:

1. **Planning and Concept Development**: How to develop a unique food truck concept that stands out in a competitive market, including defining your brand, crafting a compelling menu, and understanding your target audience.
2. **Business Essentials**: Key business considerations such as writing a business plan, securing financing, and navigating the legal and regulatory landscape.
3. **Acquiring and Outfitting Your Truck**: Tips on choosing the right vehicle, outfitting it with the necessary equipment, and ensuring compliance with health and safety standards.

4. **Operational Strategies**: Effective strategies for daily operations, inventory management, staff hiring and training, and maintaining high standards of food quality and customer service.
5. **Marketing and Growth**: Techniques for marketing your food truck, building a strong social media presence, and expanding your business through catering services, partnerships, and potential franchising opportunities.

Starting a food truck business is a rewarding endeavor that blends culinary passion with entrepreneurial zeal. As you embark on this journey, remember that success in the food truck industry requires a combination of creativity, resilience, and strategic planning. This book is here to support you every step of the way, offering guidance, encouragement, and the knowledge you need to turn your food truck dreams into a delicious reality.

Welcome to the world of food trucks—let's get rolling!

Chapter 1

Laying the Foundation

Building a successful food truck business starts with a solid foundation. This foundational phase involves detailed planning, market research, and strategic decision-making to ensure your venture has the best chance of thriving. Below, we'll carefully go through the critical elements of laying the foundation for your food truck business.

1. Concept Development: *Defining Your Vision*
The first step is to clearly define your vision. What type of cuisine will you offer? What unique angle will set your food truck apart from the competition? This vision should reflect your culinary passion and expertise while appealing to a specific market niche.

Key Considerations:
- **Cuisine and Menu:** Choose a cuisine that excites you and has potential market appeal. Develop a menu that showcases your skills and differentiates you from competitors.

- **Brand Identity**: Think about your food truck's name, logo, and overall aesthetic. Your brand should be memorable and convey the essence of your culinary offering.

- **Target Audience**: Identify your ideal customers. Are you catering to office workers, students, event-goers, or families? Understanding your target audience will guide many of your decisions.

2. Market Research: *Analyzing the Market*

Market research is crucial to validate your concept and understand the competitive landscape. Analyze local food trends, customer preferences, and the performance of existing food trucks in your area.

Key Activities:
- **Competitor Analysis**: Study other food trucks and restaurants offering similar cuisines. Note their strengths, weaknesses, and customer feedback.

- **Location Analysis**: Identify potential locations where your target audience frequents. Consider the foot traffic, demographics, and any regulatory restrictions in these areas.

- **Industry Trends**: Stay informed about trends in the food truck industry, such as popular cuisines, innovative menu items, and successful marketing strategies.

- **Customer Feedback:** Gather feedback from potential customers through surveys, focus groups, or informal conversations. This feedback will help you refine your menu and concept to better meet customer expectations.

3. Crafting a Business Plan: *Structuring Your Plan*

A comprehensive business plan is necessary for guiding your business strategy and attracting investors or securing financing. Your business plan should include the following sections:

Executive Summary: A concise overview of your business, including your concept, vision, and key objectives.

Business Description: Detailed information about your food truck, including the type of cuisine, target market, and unique selling proposition.

Market Analysis: Insights from your market research, including competitor analysis and target audience demographics.

Marketing Strategy: Plans for promoting your food truck, building a brand, and attracting and retaining customers.

Operational Plan: Details about your day-to-day operations, including sourcing ingredients, managing inventory, and ensuring food safety.

Financial Projections: Financial forecasts, including startup costs, revenue projections, and break-even analysis. This section should also outline your funding requirements and potential sources of capital.

4. Legal and Regulatory Requirements: Navigating Regulations

Operating a food truck involves complying with various local, state, and federal regulations. Research and adhere to these requirements to avoid legal issues and ensure a smooth launch.

Key Areas:

Licenses and Permits: Obtain the necessary licenses and permits, such as a business license, food handler's permit, health department permits, and parking permits.

Health and Safety Regulations: Comply with health and safety standards for food preparation, storage, and serving. Regular inspections by the health department are typically required.

Zoning Laws: Understand zoning regulations that dictate where you can park and operate your food truck. Some areas may have restrictions or designated zones for food trucks.

5. Financial Planning: *Estimating Costs*

Accurate financial planning is crucial for setting realistic expectations and securing funding. Estimate your startup costs, ongoing expenses, and potential revenue.

Key Components:

Startup Costs: Include the cost of the food truck, kitchen equipment, initial inventory, licenses and permits, branding and marketing materials, and initial working capital.

Operating Expenses: Factor in costs such as fuel, maintenance, insurance, ingredients, labor, and marketing.

Revenue Projections: Estimate your potential revenue based on your pricing strategy, target sales volume, and market demand.

6. Securing Funding

Determine how you will finance your food truck business. Options may include personal savings, loans, investor funding, or crowdfunding.

Funding Sources:

- ***Personal Savings***: Using your savings can give you full control over your business without incurring debt.

- ***Bank Loans***: Traditional bank loans or small business loans can provide substantial funding but require a solid business plan and good credit.

- ***Investors***: Attracting investors can provide capital in exchange for equity or profit sharing.

Present a compelling business plan to potential investors.

- **Crowdfunding**: Platforms like Kickstarter or Indiegogo can help you raise funds from a large number of people who believe in your concept.

7. Choosing and Outfitting Your Food Truck

Selecting the Right Vehicle

Choosing the right food truck is a critical decision. Consider factors such as size, condition, equipment needs, and budget.

Key Considerations:

Size and Layout: Ensure the truck has enough space for your equipment and staff to operate efficiently. The layout should facilitate a smooth workflow.

Condition: Decide whether to buy a new or used truck. A new truck can be customized to your needs but is more expensive. A used truck can be more affordable but may require repairs or upgrades.

Customization: Outfit your truck with the necessary kitchen equipment, storage, and serving facilities. Ensure compliance with health and safety standards.

8. Building a Strong Brand

Creating a Memorable Brand

Your brand is your identity in the market. It encompasses your name, logo, design, and overall customer experience.

Brand Elements:

Name and Logo: Choose a name that is catchy, memorable, and reflective of your cuisine. Design a logo that stands out and complements your brand.

Truck Design: Your truck's exterior design should attract attention and convey your brand's personality. Use colors, graphics, and signage that reflect your theme.

Online Presence: Establish a strong online presence through a professional website and active social media profiles. Use these platforms to engage with customers, share your story, and promote your offerings.

Laying the foundation for your food truck business involves careful planning, thorough research, and strategic decision-making. By taking the time to develop a clear concept, conduct market research, craft a comprehensive business plan, navigate legal requirements, plan your finances, choose the right vehicle, and build a strong brand, you'll be well-prepared to embark on your food truck journey. This foundational work sets the stage for operational success, helping you turn your culinary dreams into a profitable and rewarding reality.

Chapter 2

Legalities and Logistics

Navigating the Essentials of Starting a Food Truck Business

Starting a food truck business involves navigating a complex web of legal requirements and logistical considerations. Ensuring that your business is compliant with all relevant laws and regulations while efficiently managing logistical aspects is crucial for success. This chapter will guide you through the essential legalities and logistics to set a strong foundation for your food truck venture.

Legal Requirements

The first step in establishing your food truck business is to choose the appropriate business structure. This decision has significant legal and tax implications. The most common structures are sole proprietorship, partnership, limited liability company (LLC), and corporation.

- A sole proprietorship is the simplest form, offering full control to the owner but also subjecting them to personal liability.

- Partnerships share ownership and responsibilities, along with liabilities, between two or more individuals.

- An LLC provides liability protection, shielding personal assets from business debts, and offers flexible tax options.

- Corporations offer the highest level of liability protection but involve more complexity and higher costs to establish and maintain.

Once you've chosen your business structure, you need to register your business with the appropriate local, state, and federal agencies.

Begin by registering your food truck's name with your state's business authority to secure your brand identity. Then, obtain an Employer Identification Number (EIN) from the Internal Revenue Service (IRS), which is necessary for tax purposes and hiring employees.

Securing the necessary licenses and permits is another critical step. The exact requirements vary by location, but generally, you will need:

1. a business license
2. a food handler's permit
3. health department permits
4. parking permits

A business license authorizes you to operate in a specific area, while a food handler's permit ensures you and your staff are knowledgeable about safe food handling practices. Health department permits involve passing inspections to confirm your food truck meets local health and safety standards. Parking permits are essential for operating in public spaces and may be subject to zoning regulations. Compliance with health and safety regulations is paramount.

Food trucks must adhere to stringent standards for food storage, preparation, and serving to prevent foodborne illnesses. Regular inspections by the health department will be a routine part of your operation, so maintaining high standards of cleanliness and food safety is non-negotiable.

Logistical Considerations

Logistics plays a vital role in the daily operations of a food truck business. Choosing the right vehicle is a fundamental decision. Your food truck should be large enough to house all necessary equipment and accommodate staff, but not so large that it becomes difficult to maneuver or park. Consider whether you want to buy a new truck, which allows for full customization but comes at a higher cost, or a used truck, which may be more affordable but might require modifications or repairs.

Outfitting your food truck with the right equipment is essential for efficient operations. This includes cooking appliances, refrigeration units, storage solutions, and serving facilities. All equipment must comply with health and safety standards, so it's important to work with reputable suppliers and installers who understand the specific needs of food trucks.

Effective inventory management is crucial to avoid running out of ingredients or having excess that leads to waste. Establish relationships with reliable suppliers to ensure a steady supply of fresh ingredients. Implementing a robust inventory tracking system can help you monitor stock levels, manage orders, and reduce waste.

Staffing your food truck with skilled and reliable employees is another important logistical consideration. Staff should be trained not only in food preparation and safety but also in customer service. Hiring the right team can significantly impact your efficiency and customer satisfaction.

Marketing your food truck is vital to attract and retain customers. Develop a strong brand identity with a memorable name, logo, and truck design. Leverage social media platforms to build an online presence, engage with customers, and promote your locations and menu items. Participating in local events, food festivals, and markets can also increase your visibility and customer base.

Finally, understanding and complying with zoning laws is crucial for selecting operating locations.

Many cities have designated areas where food trucks can operate, and there may be restrictions on parking and serving food in certain locations. Research these regulations thoroughly and obtain any necessary permits to avoid fines or being forced to relocate.

In conclusion, laying the legal and logistical foundation for your food truck business involves careful planning and adherence to a variety of regulations and operational considerations. By choosing the right business structure, securing necessary licenses and permits, complying with health and safety standards, selecting and equipping your truck, managing inventory, staffing effectively, and marketing strategically, you can establish a robust foundation for your food truck business. This groundwork is essential for ensuring your venture operates smoothly, legally, and profitably, setting you on the path to success in the dynamic food truck industry.

Chapter 3

Designing and Outfitting your Food Truck

Designing and outfitting your food truck is a critical step in establishing your business, as it affects both functionality and customer appeal. This process involves choosing the right vehicle, customizing it to meet your specific needs, and creating a strong brand identity that attracts and retains customers.

Choosing and Customizing Your Truck

The first decision in designing your food truck is selecting the right vehicle. The size and type of truck you choose should be dictated by the nature of your business, including the menu, equipment requirements, and the number of staff members who will be working inside.

A larger truck offers more space for equipment and staff, which can increase efficiency, but it also comes with higher costs and potential difficulties in maneuvering and parking. Smaller trucks are more economical and easier to park but may limit your operational capacity.

When choosing a truck, consider whether to buy new or used. A new truck allows for complete customization and the latest technology, ensuring that all equipment is tailored to your specific needs. However, new trucks come at a higher price point. Used trucks are more affordable but might require significant modifications and repairs to meet your standards and health regulations. Regardless of the choice, ensure the vehicle is mechanically sound and compliant with local health and safety standards.

Customization is a crucial part of outfitting your food truck. The layout should be designed to facilitate a smooth workflow, maximizing efficiency during peak service times. Essential equipment includes cooking appliances such as grills, fryers, ovens, and refrigerators, along with adequate storage solutions for ingredients and utensils. It's important to install high-quality ventilation systems to maintain a safe and comfortable working environment. Additionally, ensure that all equipment is installed securely and meets health department requirements. Working with a professional who specializes in food truck outfitting can be invaluable, as they bring expertise in optimizing space and ensuring compliance with regulations.

Branding Your Food Truck

Creating a strong brand identity for your food truck is vital for standing out in a competitive market. Your brand encompasses the visual design of your truck, your logo, and the overall customer experience you provide. Start with a memorable name that reflects your cuisine and resonates with your target audience.

The name should be easy to remember and pronounce, helping potential customers recall and recommend your truck.

Your logo and truck design are the visual cornerstones of your brand. The logo should be simple yet distinctive, effectively communicating the essence of your food truck. Use colors, fonts, and imagery that align with your brand personality and appeal to your target market.

The design of the truck itself should be eye-catching and professional, creating a positive first impression. Consider a vibrant paint job, unique graphics, and clear signage that can be easily read from a distance. The exterior design should attract attention while conveying the quality and style of your food.

In addition to visual elements, branding also involves creating a consistent and enjoyable customer experience. This includes everything from the presentation of your food to the friendliness of your staff. Offering unique and high-quality menu items can help differentiate your truck and build a loyal customer base.

Engaging with customers on social media platforms can enhance your brand presence, allowing you to share updates, menu changes, and special events. Social media also provides a platform for interacting with customers, gathering feedback, and building a community around your food truck.

Moreover, consider how your brand values and story are communicated through your truck and your interactions with customers. Sharing your journey, the inspiration behind your menu, and your commitment to quality can create a deeper connection with your audience. Customers are more likely to support a business that they feel a personal connection to and that shares their values.

In summary, designing and outfitting your food truck involves a careful balance of functionality and branding. Choosing the right vehicle and customizing it to suit your operational needs ensures efficient and compliant operations. Simultaneously, developing a strong brand identity through a memorable name, distinctive logo, and engaging customer experience helps attract and retain customers. By focusing on these aspects, you can create a food truck that not only serves delicious food but also stands out in the crowded market, paving the way for long-term success.

Chapter 4

Menu Development and Operations

Launching a successful food truck business requires meticulous planning and execution, especially when it comes to menu development and day-to-day operations. This chapter delves into the critical aspects of crafting your menu, balancing creativity and cost, sourcing quality ingredients, pricing your menu items, and managing the various facets of daily operations, including inventory management, scheduling, staffing, and efficient service practices.

Crafting Your Menu

Your menu is the heart of your food truck business. It should reflect your culinary vision while catering to the tastes and preferences of your target audience. Begin by deciding on a central theme or cuisine that will define your food truck. Whether it's gourmet burgers, fusion tacos, vegan delights, or artisanal desserts, your menu should have a clear focus that sets you apart from competitors.

When crafting your menu, consider the practicality of preparing each item in a limited space with minimal equipment. Choose dishes that can be prepared quickly and consistently, ensuring that you can maintain a high level of quality during busy periods. It's also beneficial to offer a mix of popular staples and unique items that can attract a broad customer base while also enticing food enthusiasts looking for something different.

Balancing Creativity and Cost

Striking the right balance between creativity and cost is essential for a profitable menu. While innovative dishes can draw in customers, they should not compromise your bottom line. Calculate the cost of ingredients for each menu item and ensure that the selling price covers these costs while providing a healthy profit margin.

Consider seasonal variations and availability of ingredients, opting for those that are readily accessible and affordable year-round. Experiment with cost-effective ingredients that can add value and uniqueness to your menu. For instance, incorporating local produce or lesser-known cuts of meat can differentiate your offerings without breaking the bank.

Sourcing Quality Ingredients

Quality ingredients are fundamental to the success of your food truck. Establish relationships with reliable suppliers who can provide fresh, high-quality produce, meats, and other essentials. Whenever possible, source locally to ensure freshness and support your community.

Maintaining a consistent supply chain is crucial, so have backup suppliers to avoid disruptions. Regularly review and audit your suppliers to ensure they meet your standards for quality and reliability. Buying in bulk can reduce costs, but it requires careful planning and storage to prevent waste.

Pricing Your Menu Items

Pricing your menu items correctly is crucial for profitability. Conduct market research to understand the pricing landscape within your target area. Your prices should be competitive yet reflect the quality and uniqueness of your offerings.

Consider the cost of ingredients, preparation time, and overhead expenses such as labor, fuel, and maintenance. A common approach is to use a cost-plus pricing strategy, where you add a markup to the cost of producing each dish. Monitor your sales and customer feedback regularly to adjust prices if necessary, ensuring they remain fair and attractive.

Day-to-Day Operations

Effective management of day-to-day operations ensures the smooth running of your food truck. This involves planning routes, preparing ingredients in advance, and ensuring your truck is fully stocked and ready for service each day.

Start by mapping out your service areas and establishing a schedule that maximizes your presence in high-traffic locations. Consistent routines help build a loyal customer base and streamline your operations. Keep detailed records of daily sales, expenses, and inventory levels to identify trends and make informed decisions.

Inventory Management

Efficient inventory management minimizes waste and maximizes profitability. Implement a robust inventory tracking system to monitor stock levels and usage rates. Conduct regular inventory checks to ensure you have the necessary ingredients on hand and to avoid overstocking.

Organize your storage space to facilitate easy access and rotation of stock. Utilize the first-in, first-out (FIFO) method to ensure older ingredients are used before newer ones, reducing the risk of spoilage. Work closely with your suppliers to schedule timely deliveries that align with your usage patterns.

Scheduling and Staffing

Proper scheduling and staffing are vital for maintaining high service standards. Develop a staffing plan that meets your operational needs while controlling labor costs.

Consider the peak and off-peak hours of your business and schedule your staff accordingly.

Hire employees who are not only skilled in food preparation but also excel in customer service. Provide comprehensive training on your menu, preparation techniques, and safety protocols. Cross-train your staff to handle multiple roles, which adds flexibility to your team and ensures coverage during busy times or unexpected absences.

Efficient Service Practices

Efficient service practices enhance customer satisfaction and boost your operational efficiency. Design your truck layout to facilitate a smooth workflow, minimizing the time and effort required to prepare and serve each dish. Streamline your menu to focus on items that can be prepared quickly and consistently.

Adopt technology solutions like point-of-sale (POS) systems to expedite order processing and track sales data. Implement strategies for managing queues and wait times, such as taking orders from customers waiting in line or offering mobile ordering options.

Maintain clear and effective communication among your team members to ensure seamless operations. Regularly review and refine your service processes to identify and address any bottlenecks or inefficiencies.

Chapter 5

Marketing and customer engagement

Marketing and customer engagement are crucial for the success of any food truck business. With the right strategies, you can attract a steady stream of customers, build a loyal following, and distinguish your food truck from the competition. This comprehensive chapter will enlighten you about the various aspects of marketing and customer engagement, including branding, social media marketing, promotions and events, customer loyalty programs, partnerships, customer feedback, and community involvement.

Your Truck Branding

Your brand is the cornerstone of your marketing strategy. It encompasses your food truck's identity, including its name, logo, design, and the overall experience you offer to your customers. Your brand identity should reflect your unique selling proposition (USP) and resonate with your target audience. Consider the following elements when defining your brand:

- *Name*: Choose a memorable and catchy name that reflects your cuisine and personality.

- *Logo*: Design a distinctive logo that is easily recognizable and represents your brand's essence.
- *Tagline*: Create a short, impactful tagline that conveys your brand's mission and values.

- *Colors and Fonts*: Select a color palette and fonts that complement your brand's personality and appeal to your target audience.

Consistent Brand Messaging

Ensure that your brand messaging is consistent across all marketing channels. This includes your food truck's exterior, menu, website, social media profiles, and promotional materials. Consistency helps reinforce your brand identity and makes it easier for customers to recognize and remember your food truck.

Truck Design and Presentation

The design and presentation of your food truck plays a significant role in attracting customers. A visually appealing truck can draw attention and make a lasting impression. Invest in a professional design that aligns with your brand identity and ensures that your truck stands out in a crowded market. Additionally, keep your truck clean and well-maintained to convey a sense of professionalism and quality.

Social Media Marketing

Social media is a powerful tool for marketing your food truck. It allows you to reach a broad audience, engage with customers, and promote your offerings in real-time.

Choosing the Right Platforms

Identify the social media platforms that are most popular among your target audience. Common platforms for food trucks include:

- *Instagram*: Ideal for sharing high-quality photos and videos of your food, truck, and events.

- *Facebook*: Useful for creating a business page, posting updates, and engaging with customers through comments and messages.

- *Twitter*: Effective for sharing real-time updates, such as your truck's location and specials.

- *TikTok*: Great for creating short, engaging videos that showcase your food and personality.

- *Pinterest*: Useful for sharing recipes, food photography, and lifestyle content.

Creating Engaging Content

Post a variety of content to keep your audience engaged and interested. Some content ideas include:

High-Quality Photos: Share mouth-watering photos of your dishes, emphasizing the quality and presentation of your food.

Behind-the-Scenes: Give customers a glimpse into your daily operations, such as food preparation, staff interactions, and truck maintenance.

Customer Spotlights: Feature photos and stories of happy customers enjoying your food.

Promotions and Specials: Announce limited-time offers, discounts, and special menu items.

Events and Locations: Share your truck's schedule and upcoming events to keep customers informed about where they can find you.

Leveraging User-Generated Content

Encourage customers to share their experiences on social media by posting photos, reviews, and stories. User-generated content (UGC) can significantly boost your credibility and reach. Create a unique hashtag for your food truck and ask customers to use it when they post about your business. Feature UGC on your own social media profiles to show appreciation for your customers and build a sense of community.

Engaging with Your Audience

Engagement is key to building a loyal following on social media. Respond to comments, messages, and reviews promptly and professionally. Show genuine interest in your customers' feedback and experiences. Host social media contests and giveaways to encourage interaction and reward your followers.

Social Media Advertising

Consider investing in social media advertising to reach a larger audience and promote specific events or specials. Platforms like Facebook and Instagram offer targeted advertising options that allow you to reach users based on demographics, interests, and behaviors. Monitor your ad performance and adjust your strategy based on the results to maximize your return on investment.

Promotions and Events

Promotions and events are effective ways to attract new customers and keep existing ones coming back. Plan and execute various promotions and participate in local events to increase your food truck's visibility and sales.

Limited-Time Offers and Specials

Limited-time offers (LTOs) create a sense of urgency and encourage customers to try something new. Offer special menu items, discounts, or combo deals for a limited period. Promote these offers through your social media channels, website, and email newsletters to generate buzz and drive traffic to your truck.

Loyalty Programs

Implement a customer loyalty program to reward repeat customers and encourage frequent visits. Offer incentives such as discounts, free items, or exclusive access to new menu items after a certain number of purchases. Use a digital loyalty program app or physical punch cards to track customer visits and rewards.

Event Participation

Participate in local events, such as food festivals, farmers markets, and community gatherings, to increase your exposure and attract new customers. These events provide an opportunity to showcase your food, interact with potential customers, and network with other vendors. Promote your participation in events through your marketing channels to ensure your regular customers know where to find you.

Hosting Your Own Events

Consider hosting your own events to create a unique and memorable experience for your customers. Examples include:

- *Launch Parties*: Celebrate the launch of your food truck or a new menu item with a special event.

- *Themed Nights*: Host themed nights, such as Taco Tuesday or BBQ Saturdays, to attract customers looking for a specific cuisine.

- *Cooking Demonstrations*: Offer cooking demonstrations or classes to showcase your skills and engage with customers on a deeper level.

Collaborations and Partnerships

Collaborate with other local businesses, such as breweries, coffee shops, or retail stores, to cross-promote each other's offerings. These partnerships can help you reach new customers and create unique experiences. For example, partner with a brewery to offer a food and beer pairing event or collaborate with a coffee shop to create a special menu item featuring their products.

Customer Loyalty Programs

Building customer loyalty is essential for the long-term success of your food truck business. Implementing effective loyalty programs can help you retain customers, increase repeat visits, and boost overall sales.

Types of Loyalty Programs

There are several types of loyalty programs you can implement:

1. *Points-Based Programs*: Customers earn points for each purchase, which can be redeemed for discounts or free items.

2. *Punch Cards*: Customers receive a punch or stamp for each visit, with a reward given after a certain number of punches.

3. *Tiered Programs*: Customers unlock different levels of rewards based on their spending or visit frequency.

4. *Referral Programs*: Encourage customers to refer friends and family by offering rewards for successful referrals.

Implementing a Digital Loyalty Program

Digital loyalty programs are convenient and easy to manage. Several mobile apps and platforms are available that allow you to create and track loyalty programs. These apps often include features such as customer profiles, purchase history, and automated rewards. Promote your loyalty program through your marketing channels and provide clear instructions on how customers can join and participate.

Personalizing Customer Interactions

Use the data collected through your loyalty program to personalize customer interactions. Send personalized offers, birthday rewards, and thank-you messages to show appreciation for their loyalty. Personalization can enhance the customer experience and strengthen their connection to your brand.

Customer Feedback and Reviews

Customer feedback and reviews are invaluable for improving your food truck business and building trust with potential customers. Encourage feedback and actively manage your online reputation to maintain a positive image.

Encouraging Customer Feedback

Create opportunities for customers to provide feedback, both online and offline. Place a suggestion box on your food truck, include a feedback form on your website, and encourage customers to leave reviews on social media and review platforms like Yelp, Google, and TripAdvisor. Make it easy for customers to share their thoughts by providing clear instructions and links to review sites.

Responding to Reviews

Respond to all reviews, both positive and negative, in a timely and professional manner. Thank customers for their positive feedback and address any concerns or complaints raised in negative reviews. Show empathy and a willingness to resolve issues, as this demonstrates your commitment to customer satisfaction.

Using Feedback for Improvement

Analyze the feedback you receive to identify areas for improvement. Look for recurring themes or specific issues mentioned by customers and take action to address them. Implementing changes based on customer feedback can enhance your food quality, service, and overall customer experience.

Showcasing Positive Reviews

Share positive reviews and testimonials on your website, social media profiles, and marketing materials. Highlighting satisfied customers' experiences can build credibility and attract new customers. Create a dedicated section on your website for customer testimonials and encourage happy customers to share their stories.

Community Involvement

Being involved in your local community can enhance your food truck's reputation and foster strong relationships with customers. Participate in community events, support local causes, and engage with local organizations to demonstrate your commitment to the community.

Supporting Local Causes

Partner with local charities, schools, and non-profit organizations to support causes that align with your values. Donate a portion of your sales to a charity, sponsor a local event, or participate in fundraisers. Publicize your involvement through your marketing channels to show customers that you care about the community.

Participating in Community Events

Engage with your community by participating in local events such as fairs, festivals, parades, and farmers markets. These events provide opportunities to showcase your food, interact with potential customers, and build brand awareness. Promote your participation in community events on your social media profiles and website.

Hosting Community Events

Host your own community events to bring people together and create memorable experiences. Consider organizing food drives, cooking competitions, or family-friendly gatherings. These events can strengthen your connection to the community and provide additional marketing opportunities.

Collaborating with Local Businesses

Build relationships with other local businesses to create mutually beneficial partnerships. Collaborate on joint promotions, events, or cross-marketing efforts to expand your reach and attract new customers. For example, partner with a local coffee shop to offer a breakfast combo or work with a nearby brewery to create a food and beer pairing event.

Marketing Analytics and Measurement

Monitoring the effectiveness of your marketing efforts is essential for making informed decisions and optimizing your strategies. Use marketing analytics and measurement tools to track your performance and identify areas for improvement.

Setting Marketing Goals

Establish clear marketing goals that align with your overall business objectives. These goals might include increasing brand awareness, driving more foot traffic, boosting sales, or growing your social media following. Setting specific, measurable, achievable, relevant, and time-bound (SMART) goals will help you stay focused and track your progress.

Tracking Key Metrics

Identify key performance indicators (KPIs) to measure the success of your marketing efforts. Common KPIs for food trucks include:

- *Sales Revenue*: Track your daily, weekly, and monthly sales to gauge overall performance.

- *Customer Acquisition*: Monitor the number of new customers you attract through your marketing efforts.

- *Customer Retention*: Measure the percentage of repeat customers and their frequency of visits.

- **Social Media Engagement**: Track metrics such as likes, comments, shares, and follower growth on your social media profiles.

- **Website Traffic**: Use tools like Google Analytics to monitor website traffic, page views, and user behavior.

- **Email Marketing Performance**: Analyze open rates, click-through rates, and conversion rates for your email campaigns.

Analyzing Data and Making Adjustments

Regularly review your marketing analytics to assess the effectiveness of your strategies. Identify trends, strengths, and areas for improvement. Use this data to make informed adjustments to your marketing plan, such as reallocating your budget, refining your messaging, or experimenting with new tactics.

A/B Testing

Conduct A/B testing to compare different marketing approaches and determine which ones yield the best results. Test variables such as ad copy, visuals, promotional offers, and social media content. Analyze the results to identify the most effective strategies and optimize your campaigns accordingly.

Digital Marketing Strategies

In addition to social media marketing, leverage other digital marketing strategies to expand your reach and attract more customers.

Search Engine Optimization (SEO)

Optimize your website and online content to improve your search engine rankings. This makes it easier for potential customers to find your food truck when searching for relevant keywords. Key SEO practices include:

Keyword Research: Identify and incorporate relevant keywords into your website content, blog posts, and meta descriptions.

On-Page Optimization: Ensure your website is mobile-friendly, has fast loading times, and includes clear, concise content with relevant keywords.

Local SEO: Optimize your Google My Business listing, including accurate contact information, business hours, and customer reviews.

Content Marketing

Create valuable and engaging content to attract and retain customers. Content marketing can take various forms, such as blog posts, videos, recipes, and how-to guides. Share your content on your website, social media profiles, and email newsletters to provide value to your audience and establish your food truck as an authority in your niche.

Email Marketing

Build an email list and use email marketing to keep your customers informed and engaged. Send regular newsletters featuring updates, promotions, and exclusive offers. Personalize your emails to make them more relevant to your subscribers and encourage them to visit your food truck.

Online Advertising

Invest in online advertising to reach a larger audience and drive traffic to your food truck. Consider platforms such as Google Ads, Facebook Ads, and Instagram Ads, which offer targeted advertising options based on demographics, interests, and behaviors. Monitor your ad performance and adjust your campaigns to maximize their effectiveness.

Offline Marketing Strategies

While digital marketing is essential, offline marketing strategies can also play a significant role in promoting your food truck and engaging with customers.

Flyers and Posters

Distribute flyers and posters in high-traffic areas, such as community centers, gyms, coffee shops, and college campuses. Include eye-catching visuals, a clear message, and your food truck's location, operating hours, and contact information. Offer a discount or special offer on the flyer to incentivize customers to visit your truck.

Business Cards

Hand out business cards to customers, partners, and potential clients. Ensure your cards include your food truck's name, logo, contact information, and social media profiles. Business cards are a professional way to make a lasting impression and encourage repeat business.

Local Media

Reach out to local media outlets, such as newspapers, magazines, radio stations, and TV channels, to share your food truck's story and promote your offerings. Offer to provide samples of your food for a feature or interview. Local media coverage can significantly boost your visibility and attract new customers.

Networking

Build relationships with other food truck owners, restaurant owners, and industry professionals. Attend industry events, join local business associations, and participate in networking groups. Networking can provide valuable insights, opportunities for collaboration, and referrals.

Sponsorships and Donations

Sponsor local events, sports teams, or community initiatives to increase your visibility and demonstrate your support for the community. Offer food donations for charity events, school functions, or nonprofit organizations. Sponsorships and donations can create positive associations with your brand and attract new customers.

Customer Engagement Techniques

Engaging with your customers is crucial for building strong relationships and fostering loyalty. Implement various techniques to enhance customer engagement and create memorable experiences.

Personalization

Personalize your interactions with customers to make them feel valued and appreciated. Address customers by name, remember their favorite orders, and offer personalized recommendations based on their preferences. Personalization can significantly enhance the customer experience and encourage repeat business.

Customer Surveys

Conduct customer surveys to gather feedback on their experiences, preferences, and suggestions for improvement. Use this feedback to make informed decisions about your menu, service, and marketing strategies. Show customers that you value their opinions by implementing changes based on their feedback.

Interactive Experiences

Create interactive experiences for your customers to enhance their engagement with your brand. Examples include:

- *Cooking Demonstrations*: Host live cooking demonstrations or classes to showcase your skills and interact with customers.

- *Photo Opportunities*: Set up photo booths or designated photo spots with branded props and backdrops to encourage customers to take and share photos.

- *Games and Contests*: Organize games, contests, or trivia nights to entertain customers and encourage participation.

Customer Appreciation Events

Host customer appreciation events to show gratitude for your loyal customers. Offer special discounts, free samples, or exclusive access to new menu items. Use these events to engage with customers, gather feedback, and strengthen your relationships.

Exceptional Customer Service

Provide exceptional customer service to create positive experiences and build lasting relationships. Train your staff to be friendly, attentive, and responsive to customer needs. Address any issues or complaints promptly and professionally to demonstrate your commitment to customer satisfaction.

Chapter 6

Growth Strategies and Financial Management of a Food Truck Business

The food truck industry has seen remarkable growth over the past decade, emerging as a popular and viable option for culinary entrepreneurs. The allure of this business model lies in its mobility, relatively low startup costs compared to traditional brick-and-mortar restaurants, and the flexibility to offer a variety of innovative food options. Despite these advantages, achieving long-term success requires food truck owners to implement effective growth strategies and maintain robust financial management practices.

Growth Strategies

Market Research and Niche Identification

A crucial first step in establishing a successful food truck business is conducting thorough market research. This involves understanding the demographics, preferences, and spending habits of your target audience. Identifying who your customers are will guide your business decisions and help tailor your offerings to meet their needs.

Choosing a specific niche is equally important. By specializing in a unique cuisine, dietary focus (such as vegan or gluten-free options), or a particular meal type (such as breakfast or desserts), you can differentiate your food truck from competitors and build a loyal customer base.

Strategic Location Planning

The location of your food truck significantly impacts its success. Positioning your truck in high-traffic areas such as business districts, parks, and nightlife hotspots can attract a steady stream of customers. Participating in local events, festivals, and farmers' markets can further increase your visibility and help you reach new customers. Developing a rotating location schedule allows you to tap into different customer bases on different days, maximizing your reach and preventing market saturation in any single area.

Branding and Marketing

Creating a strong brand identity is essential for attracting and retaining customers. This involves developing a memorable name, logo, and consistent visual elements that reflect your business's personality and values. An active social media presence is crucial in today's digital age. Platforms like Instagram, Facebook, and Twitter can be used to engage with customers, share your location, promote special events, and gather valuable feedback. Partnering with local influencers and food bloggers can enhance your exposure and credibility, while loyalty programs can encourage repeat business by rewarding customers for their patronage.

Menu Innovation

Keeping your menu fresh and exciting is vital for maintaining customer interest and satisfaction. Offering seasonal items allows you to capitalize on seasonal ingredients and trends, providing customers with new and interesting options.

Regularly soliciting and incorporating customer feedback can help you improve and evolve your offerings to meet their preferences. Special promotions and limited-time offers can attract new customers and reward loyal ones, creating a sense of urgency and excitement around your food truck.

Expansion and Diversification

Once your initial truck achieves success, consider expanding with additional trucks in new locations to reach a broader audience. Offering catering services for private events such as weddings, corporate gatherings, and parties can diversify your revenue streams and increase brand awareness.

If your brand gains significant popularity, you might explore the possibility of opening a brick-and-mortar restaurant to complement your food truck business, providing a stable and permanent location for your loyal customers.

Financial Management

Budgeting and Forecasting

Effective financial management begins with detailed budgeting and forecasting. Clearly outlining all initial expenses, including the cost of the truck, equipment, permits, and initial inventory, helps ensure you have adequate capital to start your business.

Developing a comprehensive operating budget that includes both fixed costs (such as loan payments and insurance) and variable costs (such as ingredients and fuel) is crucial for managing day-to-day operations. Estimating revenue based on realistic sales projections and historical data, if available, allows you to set achievable financial goals and monitor your progress.

Cost Control

Controlling costs is essential for maintaining profitability. Implementing an efficient inventory management system can help reduce waste and control food costs, ensuring you only purchase what you need. Building strong relationships with suppliers can lead to better prices and terms, while bulk purchasing can result in cost savings. Regularly reviewing and analyzing expenses helps identify areas where you can cut costs without compromising quality, allowing you to operate more efficiently.

Pricing Strategy

Developing a competitive pricing strategy involves conducting market research to understand the pricing strategies of competitors.

This information helps you set prices that are attractive to customers while ensuring you cover costs and achieve a reasonable profit margin. Offering value through high-quality ingredients, generous portions, and excellent customer service can justify higher prices and enhance customer satisfaction.

Cash Flow Management

Maintaining positive cash flow is critical for the sustainability of your food truck business. Monitoring cash flow on a regular basis allows you to anticipate and address any shortfalls before they become problematic. Establishing a cash reserve can provide a financial cushion for unexpected expenses or slow periods. Implementing efficient payment processing systems can also help improve cash flow by ensuring timely collection of revenues.

Financial Reporting and Analysis

Regular financial reporting and analysis provide insights into the performance of your business and inform strategic decisions. Preparing and reviewing financial statements such as profit and loss statements, balance sheets, and cash flow statements on a monthly or quarterly basis allows you to track your financial health. Conducting variance analysis to compare actual results against budgeted figures helps identify areas where performance can be improved.

Tax Compliance and Planning

Ensuring compliance with all tax obligations is essential to avoid penalties and legal issues. Keeping accurate records of all income and expenses, and working with a knowledgeable accountant or tax professional, can help you navigate the complexities of tax regulations.

Planning for tax obligations in advance ensures you set aside sufficient funds to meet your liabilities.

In conclusion, the growth and financial management of a food truck business require careful planning, strategic execution, and continuous monitoring. By implementing effective growth strategies and maintaining robust financial practices, food truck owners can build successful and sustainable businesses that thrive in a competitive and dynamic industry.

CONCLUSION

The Road Ahead

Embarking on the journey of starting a food truck business is an exciting and rewarding endeavor. The road ahead is filled with opportunities to explore new culinary horizons, connect with diverse communities, and build a brand that resonates with customers. While the path may be challenging, the potential for growth and success is immense for those who approach it with passion, creativity, and a strategic mindset.

The allure of the food truck industry lies in its dynamism and flexibility. Unlike traditional restaurants, food trucks can adapt quickly to changing market trends, shifting consumer preferences, and emerging opportunities.

This agility allows you to experiment with different menu items, locations, and marketing strategies, enabling you to find the perfect formula for success. Embrace this flexibility and use it to your advantage by staying attuned to the latest food trends and continually refining your offerings.

One of the most fulfilling aspects of running a food truck is the direct connection you forge with your customers. Every interaction is an opportunity to create a memorable experience, whether through exceptional customer service, unique culinary creations, or engaging social media content. Building strong relationships with your customers not only fosters loyalty but also generates invaluable word-of-mouth marketing. Your ability to create a community around your food truck can be a powerful driver of long-term success.

Financial management is a cornerstone of any successful business, and the food truck industry is no exception. By maintaining a meticulous approach to budgeting, cost control, and cash flow management, you can ensure that your business remains financially healthy.

This financial discipline will empower you to invest in growth opportunities, whether it's expanding your fleet, offering catering services, or even opening a brick-and-mortar restaurant in the future. Remember, every dollar saved through efficient management is a dollar that can be reinvested into your business to fuel further growth.

Innovation and adaptability are your best allies in this journey. The food truck landscape is competitive, but it's also ripe with potential for those who are willing to think outside the box. Continually seek ways to differentiate your business, whether through unique menu items, compelling branding, or exceptional customer experiences. Stay open to feedback and be willing to pivot when necessary.

The ability to innovate and adapt will not only help you overcome challenges but also position your business for sustained success in an ever-evolving market.

As you navigate the road ahead, it's important to stay motivated and resilient. There will be obstacles and setbacks, but each challenge presents an opportunity to learn and grow. Surround yourself with a supportive network of fellow entrepreneurs, mentors, and advisors who can offer guidance and encouragement.

Celebrate your successes, no matter how small, and use them as fuel to keep pushing forward. Your passion for food and dedication to your craft will be the driving force behind your success.

Conclusively, the journey of starting and growing a food truck business is a remarkable adventure filled with endless possibilities. With a clear vision, strategic planning, and a relentless commitment to excellence, you can turn your culinary dreams into reality. Embrace the opportunities, overcome the challenges, and savor every moment of the ride.

The road ahead is yours to conquer, and the future of your food truck business is as bright as you dare to dream.

Sample Food Truck Business Plan

Executive Summary
Business Name: Savory SteerFood Truck

Owner: Jane Doe

Location: Metropolitan City, Various Locations

Business Concept: Savory Steer Food Truck will offer gourmet street food with a focus on high-quality ingredients, creative menu items, and exceptional customer service. Our primary cuisine will be a fusion of modern American and international street foods, targeting food enthusiasts and professionals in the bustling city environment.

Mission Statement: Our mission is to provide delicious, high-quality, and innovative street food to the people of Metropolitan City, while offering an exceptional dining experience that creates lasting memories.

Objectives:
- Establish a recognizable and reputable food truck brand in Metropolitan City.
- Achieve a daily sales target of $1,500 within the first six months.
- Expand to three food trucks within five years.

- Introduce catering services within two years.

Company Description

Urban Bites Food Truck will serve the busy streets of Metropolitan City, offering a variety of gourmet street foods that blend modern American and international flavors. Our business will operate in high-traffic areas, at events, and through catering services. We aim to provide a unique and delightful culinary experience, with a commitment to quality and customer satisfaction.

**Legal Structure*:* Urban Bites Food Truck will be registered as a Limited Liability Company (LLC) to provide personal liability protection for the owner.

Market Analysis

**Industry Overview*:* The food truck industry has seen significant growth, driven by consumer demand for convenient, high-quality, and diverse food options. The industry is projected to continue its upward trend, especially in urban areas with dense populations and vibrant food cultures.

**Target Market*:* Our primary target market consists of young professionals, students, and food enthusiasts aged 18-45 who are seeking quick, tasty, and unique dining options. We will focus on high-traffic areas such as business districts, college campuses, parks, and popular event venues.

Market Needs: There is a strong demand for convenient yet high-quality food options in Metropolitan City. Customers are looking for unique and innovative flavors, healthy and sustainable ingredients, and a memorable dining experience.

Competitive Analysis: Key competitors include other food trucks offering gourmet and ethnic foods, fast-casual restaurants, and local eateries. Urban Bites Food Truck will differentiate itself through its fusion cuisine, exceptional customer service, and strategic location planning.

Marketing Strategy
Branding: The Urban Bites brand will be synonymous with quality, innovation, and a delightful dining experience. Our logo, truck design, and marketing materials will reflect our modern and creative approach to street food.

Promotion:
Social Media: Active presence on Instagram, Facebook, and Twitter to engage with customers, share daily locations, promote special events, and gather feedback.

Influencer Partnerships: Collaborate with local food bloggers and social media influencers to increase brand visibility and credibility.

Events and Festivals: Participate in local food festivals, markets, and community events to reach a broader audience and build brand awareness.

Loyalty Program: Implement a digital loyalty program to reward repeat customers with discounts and special offers.

Sales Strategy:

Daily Operations: Operate in high-traffic areas during peak meal times (lunch and dinner).

Catering Services: Offer catering for private events, corporate gatherings, and parties to diversify revenue streams.

Online Ordering: Partner with food delivery platforms to provide convenient online ordering and delivery options.

Menu and Services
Core Menu Items:

Fusion Tacos: Soft corn tortillas filled with a variety of international flavors such as Korean BBQ beef, Thai chicken, and Mediterranean falafel.

Gourmet Burgers: Unique burger creations using premium beef, chicken, and vegetarian patties with innovative toppings.

Loaded Fries: Fresh-cut fries topped with a variety of gourmet toppings like truffle oil, Parmesan cheese, and spicy aioli.

Seasonal Specials: Rotating menu items based on seasonal ingredients and customer feedback.

Beverages: A selection of craft sodas, freshly squeezed juices, and specialty coffees.

Operational Plan
Location Strategy:

Daily Schedule: Develop a weekly schedule to operate in different high-traffic locations each day.

Event Participation: Secure permits and vendor spots at local festivals, markets, and events.
Catering: Develop a catering menu and marketing materials to promote services for private events.

Staffing:
Initial Team: Hire a small team of experienced cooks and customer service staff.

Training: Provide thorough training on food preparation, safety, and customer service.

Growth: Plan for additional hires as the business expands and demand increases.

Suppliers:
Local Sourcing: Partner with local farmers and suppliers to source fresh, high-quality ingredients.
Sustainable Practices: Implement sustainable sourcing and waste management practices to reduce environmental impact.

Financial Plan
Startup Costs:

Food Truck: $80,000 (includes truck purchase and initial customization)

Equipment and Supplies: $15,000 (cooking equipment, utensils, packaging)

Licenses and Permits: $5,000 (business license, health permits, parking permits)

Initial Inventory: $5,000 (food and beverage inventory)

Marketing and Branding: $5,000 (website, logo, promotional materials)

Working Capital: $20,000 (operating expenses for the first three months)
- **Total Startup Costs:** $130,000
- **Revenue Projections:**
- **Daily Sales Target:** $1,500

- **Monthly Sales Target:** $45,000
- **Annual Sales Target:** $540,000
- **Expense Projections:**
- **Monthly Fixed Costs:** $10,000 (loan payments, insurance, permits)
- **Monthly Variable Costs:** $25,000 (ingredients, fuel, staff wages)
- **Total Monthly Costs:** $35,000
- **Profit Projections:**
- **Monthly Profit:** $10,000
- **Annual Profit:** $120,000
- **Break-Even Analysis:**
- **Break-Even Point:** $1,167 per day (calculated by dividing total monthly costs by the number of operating days per month)

Funding Requirements: Savory Steer Food Truck seeks an initial investment of $130,000 to cover startup costs. Funding will be obtained through a combination of personal savings, a small business loan, and potential investors.

Appendix

Legal Documentation: Copies of business licenses, permits, and insurance policies.

Menu Samples: Detailed descriptions and pricing of core menu items and seasonal specials.

Vendor Agreements: Contracts and agreements with suppliers for ingredients and equipment.

Financial Statements: Pro forma income statements, balance sheets, and cash flow statements for the first three years.

Conclusion

Savory Steer Food Truck is poised to capture a significant share of the gourmet street food market in Metropolitan City. With a strong business concept, a strategic marketing plan, and a commitment to quality and customer satisfaction, we are confident in our ability to achieve our goals and create a successful and sustainable business. The road ahead is full of exciting opportunities, and we are ready to embark on this culinary journey with passion and determination.

Glossary of Terms

A

Advertising: The process of promoting your food truck through various media channels to attract customers.

Asset: Any resource owned by the food truck business that has economic value, such as the truck itself, equipment, and inventory.

B

Branding: The process of creating a unique identity for your food truck through logos, colors, and marketing strategies to distinguish it from competitors.

Break-Even Point: The point at which total revenue equals total expenses, meaning the business is not making a profit or loss.

C

Cash Flow: The net amount of cash being transferred into and out of the business, crucial for maintaining operations and covering expenses.

Catering: Providing food services for private events, such as weddings, parties, or corporate gatherings, often as an additional revenue stream for a food truck.

Commissionary *Kitchen*: A shared commercial kitchen space where food truck operators can prepare and store their food before loading it onto their trucks.

D

Depreciation: The process of allocating the cost of a tangible asset over its useful life, such as a food truck or kitchen equipment.

Dry Storage: Storage areas designated for non-perishable food items and supplies, such as canned goods, spices, and paper products.

E

Employee Identification Number (EIN): A unique number assigned by the IRS to identify a business entity for tax purposes.

Equipment: Tools and machinery necessary for food preparation and service, such as grills, fryers, refrigerators, and POS systems.

F

Fixed Costs: Business expenses that remain constant regardless of the level of production or sales, such as insurance, permits, and loan payments.

Food Cost: The total cost of ingredients used to prepare the food, a critical factor in pricing menu items and managing profitability.

G

Gross Profit: The difference between total revenue and the cost of goods sold (COGS), before accounting for operating expenses.

H

Health Inspection: A mandatory evaluation conducted by local health authorities to ensure food trucks meet sanitary and food safety standards.

HACCP (Hazard Analysis and Critical Control Points): A systematic approach to food safety that identifies and addresses potential hazards in food production and handling.

I

Inventory Management: The process of ordering, storing, and using a business's inventory, including raw materials, components, and finished products.

Insurance: Various types of coverage required to protect the food truck business, including liability, vehicle, and workers' compensation insurance.

L

License: Official permission granted by local authorities to operate a food truck, including business licenses and health permits.

Liability: Legal responsibility for any damages or injuries caused by the business operations, typically covered by insurance.

M

Marketing: Activities and strategies used to promote the food truck, attract customers, and increase sales, such as social media, flyers, and events.

Menu Engineering: The strategic design and pricing of a menu to maximize profitability and popularity of items.

N

Net Profit: The amount of money left after all expenses, including COGS, operating expenses, and taxes, have been deducted from total revenue.

O

Operating Costs: The day-to-day expenses required to run the food truck, including food, fuel, labor, and maintenance.

Overhead: The ongoing expenses of operating a business that are not directly tied to producing goods or services, such as rent, utilities, and administrative costs.

P

Permits: Official documents required by local government agencies to operate a food truck, including health permits, parking permits, and vendor licenses.

Point of Sale (POS) System: Technology used to process customer transactions, manage sales, and track inventory.

R

Revenue: The total income generated from selling food and services before any expenses are deducted.

Rotating Location Schedule: A strategy where a food truck changes its location on a regular basis to reach different customer bases and maximize exposure.

S

Sanitation: Practices and procedures followed to ensure cleanliness and hygiene in food preparation and service areas, crucial for health compliance.

Seasonal Menu: Menu items that change based on seasonal availability of ingredients, often used to keep offerings fresh and exciting.

T

Target Market: The specific group of consumers that a food truck aims to serve, defined by demographics, preferences, and behavior.

Truck Maintenance: Regular upkeep and repairs needed to keep the food truck operational, including engine checks, tire replacements, and kitchen equipment servicing.

U

Utilities: Essential services required to operate the food truck, such as electricity, water, and gas.

V

Variable Costs: Expenses that fluctuate based on the level of production or sales, such as food ingredients and packaging materials.

W

Waste Management: Practices for minimizing and disposing of food and packaging waste, including recycling and composting programs.

Working Capital: The funds available to cover day-to-day operations and short-term obligations, calculated as current assets minus current liabilities.

Z

Zoning Regulations: Local laws and ordinances that govern where food trucks can park and operate, often dictating permissible locations and hours of operation.

www.ingramcontent.com/pod-product-compliance
Lightning Source LLC
Chambersburg PA
CBHW071836210526
45479CB00001B/155